HOW TO SELL YOUR BUSINESS IN KENT & SUSSEX

ALEX PAWLE

KENT BUSINESS INVESTORS

LET'S INVEST IN INDUSTRY

CONTENTS

INTRODUCTION

As a Kent-based business owner this is the book I wish I had read before embarking on my journey to sell my business. We business owners are under-trained on such an important event in our lives.

When you are a business owner you understand sales, product, hiring good staff and building culture. However selling one's business is a unique experience, which typically only occurs once in a business owner's life. Can you therefore imagine how much pressure to perform there is when a shareholder sells his most valuable asset, after many years working in and on the business, for a large amount of money, and with no clear understanding of the process?

Granted, I am not a professional adviser, a solicitor, or an M&A investment banker. But I have gone through the same process you are going to go through, at some point in your life. Thank you for picking up this book and investing your time in understanding how a business sale works. As with all practical knowledge, I aim to help you to reduce the probability of making bad decisions during your sale process.

In the end game, what is good for you is good for county and country: making sure that SMEs, the backbone of our economy and the main source of its jobs, are handed from one generation to the next to make sure skills, jobs and profits are preserved and maintained.

You will find several contributions from local advisers and experts, who have expert knowledge of many different aspects of building a valuable company based down the road, they have deep expertise and will offer good advice. I have always felt I have grown more rapidly in my personal journey every time I accepted to take the advice of someone who had been there and done that before me.

I sold my own business, Mot-Tech, in June 2019, for the proverbial undisclosed sum. I coinvest with my friend Stephane Leduc, a business owner based in Kent having sold his company to book publishing giant Albin Michel in December 2018. We are both now reinvesting the proceeds of our respective share sales in the acquisition of industrial SMEs in Kent and East Sussex. Our tag line is: "Let's invest in industry". Let's invest in Britain's industrial talent and companies. Industry brings great jobs and wealth to our communities.

Write to me at a.pawle@kentbusinessinvestors.co.uk if you want to get in touch. After all, I am based just down the road.

Alex Pawle
Kent Business Investors
01227 314 072

CHAPTER ONE

WHEN TO SELL

The downside of just keeping it

If you own a business and have considered selling your company, you may be aware of the value of your business to would-be acquirers. According to the latest analysis, the average offer being made by acquirers is 3 times your pre-tax profit. Companies with less than a million pounds in profit can expect 3-4x multiples, and larger businesses over 1 million pounds in profits may get closer to five times the pre-tax profit but, regardless of size, private company multiples are still significantly less than those reserved for quoted companies.

You may be tempted to hold on to your business and keep it for decades to come. After all, you might reason that if you hang onto your business for four or five more years, you could withdraw the same amount in dividends as you would get from a sale and still own 100% of the business. However some risks are involved in this strategy.

You bear the Risk

The biggest downside of holding on to your business rather than selling it, is that you keep all the risks. Most entrepreneurs have an optimism bias, but you need only remember how life felt in 2008 and in the following years to be reminded that economic cycles go in both directions. As I write these lines Brexit is a few months away, we are in the middle of a global pandemic, and who knows what is in store for British businesses?

Random Access Memory

If you think of your brain like a computer, owning a business is like constantly using 95% of your RAM and processor capacity. Yes, in theory you can do other things like play golf or enjoy a bicycle trip through Tuscany and still own your business, but as long as you are the owner, your business will always occupy a large chunk of your brain's capacity. This means family fun, holidays and weekends are always tainted with the background hum of your brain's operating system churning through data. You carry with you the heavy burden of being responsible for all those jobs.

Asset intensive businesses

Let's say your business generates £500,000 in profit before tax, and you could sell your company for three times PBT or keep it. You may argue it's better to keep it, pull your profit out in the form of dividends, and capture the same cash in four years as you would by selling it. But this doesn't hold water if you have a lot of Capital Expenditures to make. If you have to buy machines, finance your customers, or stock, a lot of your cash will be locked up in feeding your business, and the amount of cash you can pull out of your business each year is a fraction of your EBITDA.

Tax Treatment

In the UK, the sale proceeds of your business will be more favourably treated than income you would receive by paying yourself handsomely with the Just Keep It Strategy. You may have to pay yourself an income of £2 or £3 for every £1 you can net from the advantageous tax treatment of a business sale.

You Can Do Better

Finally, you may be able to attract an offer higher than two, three, or four times your pre-tax profit. The businesses who work on optimising their exit get offers based on higher multiples of their pre-tax profit. Some owners do even better, stretching multiples into double digits.

The right figure

We all have a different risk appetite. Let's say you have a business worth £1 million today. Would you be willing to risk the entire thing on a new strategy in order to make a shot at making it into a £10 million company? Many entrepreneurs would take that bet.

Now imagine you have a company worth £10 million and your business represents the bulk of your net worth. Most would argue £10 million is life-changing money. Would you be willing to risk your entire company for a chance to make it a £100 million company? The marginal utility of an extra £90 million is minimal - we all only need so many Jaguars - but the risk is significant. Fewer owners would bet £10 million for a chance at £100 million.

What if your business was worth £100 million? Would you risk it all for a long shot at becoming a billion-pound company? It is hard to imagine any one person betting £100 million on anything, but if you're the MD of a billion-pound company with ambitious growth goals, £100 million is a bet you may be willing to make. When someone else is willing to invest more in your business than you are, it is probably time for your company to find a new owner. The buyer needs to see your company as a self-sustaining entity, managed and operated by professionals paid at market value.

CHAPTER TWO

PREPARE YOUR BUSINESS FOR SALE

Make sure the business operates independently of its shareholders

Your business needs to be able to operate without you, and without any of your partners or family members who would have had to leave upon the sale of the business. Not only should the business be able to remain in operation, but, after you leave, it also needs to be as profitable and be maintain the same level of sales. Think of whether you play a key role in any of the company's processes: are you a key salesperson, a key relationship manager, the holder of the keys to the IT system, etc.? Extricate yourself from the key processes of the company by delegating these jobs to your staff or to third party contractors, or by training your existing human resources so that they can operate at the same high level to which you had become accustomed.

The buyer's perspective

Why is this so important? Let's take the buyer's perspective. The investor is looking for a cash-flow generating asset. Some investors acquire property, others acquire PLC shares, and others acquire small businesses.

All investors are ultimately after the cash flow generated by a particular asset. Imagine that investors are in a shop selling cash-flow machines. Your business is one such cash-flow machine, with its characteristics, sitting on a shelf next to other cash-flow machines.

The cost of an asset is typically linked to the risk associated with the cash flow it generates. For example, as the cash flow generated by a property is typically low risk (you can always find a council to rent your residential property in the UK, for instance), the cost of the asset is high, which in turn leads to a low return on investment. The risk that a share in the FTSE 100 index will drastically change its dividend policy, or that the value of the asset sinks is also quite low, hence the cost of PLC-quoted shares is very high (the value of the asset in relation to cash flow is called the Price-Earnings ratio (P/E ratio), which is typically 10x-20x on the stock exchange.)

On the other hand, the risk that your small business has a bad year, with a lower turnover, or a fall in profits, is very high. Hence the value to an investor of the profits generated by a small company is typically much lower than equivalent profits generated by a property or by a PLC. The buyer will want to compensate this risk with several reassurances. He will want to make sure: that the cash flow is stable and will always be more than sufficient to reimburse the acquisition debt; that the business is not going to disappear after you leave; that the skills of the business are not concentrated in the hands of a few key people whose loss would devastate the company; that the firm is not overly dependent on a few large customers.

As you can see, the buyer's concern is that the business continues to operate smoothly. Reassuring the buyer that your business can operate without you will provide reassurance both to the investor and to the lender.

WHAT DO THE SHARPEST BUSINESS OWNERS WANT?

What is your company's goal for the year? Most have us have a profit-related target. While these goals are critical, there is another objective that may have even bigger consequences: building a business which can be sold. But what if you don't want to sell? That's irrelevant. Here are five reasons why building a sellable business should be your most important goal, regardless of when you plan to exit:

1. If you can sell, you're free
One of the main elements of the ability to sell your business is how it would fare if you were unable to work for some time. As long as your company is dependent on you, you don't really have a sellable business. Your goal should be to make your company less dependent on you by building a management team and creating continuously improving systems which your staff can follow. This will allow you to spend time away from your company. Think of the benefits arising, as a consequence of your choice, from not going into the office tomorrow.

2. Enjoy business more with one that operates without you
Running your business would be a more enjoyable activity if you were able to spend your days on strategic thinking. Instead, most owner operators of businesses spend most of their day on micro management: filling in forms, HR, bank statements, bookkeeping, customer issues, chasing expense receipts. The uninteresting details of owning a company remove the enjoyment in it - these are the tasks you need to get someone else to do if you're ever going to sell.

3. The ability to sell means financial independence
Each month you open your pension fund statement or your share account to see how your portfolio is doing. Not because you want to sell your shares, but because you want to know where you stand on the journey to financial freedom. Creating a sellable business also allows you peace of mind, knowing that you're building something that - just like your share portfolio - has a value you could choose to make liquid one day.

4. The ability to sell is an investment in your family

Imagine that your daughter graduates from the University of Kent, and as a gift you give her your 1975 Triumph Stag. She takes it for a drive, but after a few miles, the engine starts smoking. The mechanic takes one look under the hood and declares that the radiator has bust, and the engine needs a rebuild. You thought you were giving your daughter a beautiful asset, but instead it is an expensive liability she can't afford to keep, and which she can't sell either without feeling guilty. You may be planning to leave your business to your children or let your young managers buy into your company over time. These are both options that make a lot of sense, but if your business is too dependent on you, and it hasn't been structured to operate without you, you may be handing over a burden.

5. The Mythical Man-Month

Some things in life take time, no matter how much you want do them in a rush. Making your business sellable often requires significant changes; and a prospective buyer will want to see how your business has performed in the three years following the changes required. Therefore, if you want to sell in five years, you need to start making your business sellable now, so that the changes have time to become infused throughout your organisation.

Hire a sales team

You may be the business's only salesperson and you may want to keep for yourself the most strategic contacts. You may have relationships that stretch back to the foundation of the company, with clients who helped you set it up with you as your own boss. In the company I recently sold, 16 years after its foundation, we still work for our first client, an international news agency. Although I, as an individual, have a great relationship with the client's representative, many years ago, the main point of contact had ceased to be me or my partner. Hence, the client saw no difference when I ceased to be involved in my company.

But imagine how your buyer would perceive the same company if the representative of one of your largest clients was your golf buddy, whom you knew socially, and who was loyal to you personally. He would think that when you leave the company, it would not be disloyal to you to choose another provider. This is understandably a worrying perspective for the buyer.

It can also be a source of worry to imagine that you will set up shop down the road and divert your old clients to your new business as soon as your shares are sold. Typically, however, the sale and purchase agreement will include a non-compete clause, preventing you from working in the same industry, for a given time, within a given geographic range.

Hence, to maximise the value of your business you need to prove that you are not the main salesperson, and that the key relationships with your clients will not be altered after the sale.

In order to prove that your company, rather than you, has set up a strong series of relationships with your clients, there is nothing better than a CRM. Customer Relationship Management software can help you prove to your buyer that it is your team and not you that is in charge of the relationships that have been developed with your clients.

In addition to strong client relationships, the value of your company will be enhanced if your company knows that you have a marketing process that generates leads that continue in your absence. This marketing machine is basically a system for generating new leads, day in, day out. It can be as simple as an advertising contract in a trade journal, or as sophisticated as monthly direct mail, or a website conversion funnel. Imagine the buyer's interest when he sees that the complex task of finding new clients is integrated into the business he is buying!

Make sure your business is processed

If I only had one book that I would like to recommend to a business owner looking to sell their business, it would be 'The E-Myth.' The author, Michael Gerber, explains why most businesses get stuck or fail, and thus never get sold.

As Michael Gerber puts it, "Where were you before you started your business?" In most cases, the answer he found was that the person running the business was previously working for someone else. He started the business due to an 'Entrepreneurial Seizure' which was based on a fatal assumption that: "If you understand the technical work of a business, you understand the business that does the technical work." But this assumption is false! When you are a business owner, you need to play multiple roles at a time. This is what most people fail to do and that is the answer why their business gets stuck or shut down at the end, instead of getting sold.

According to Gerber, you need to play three roles at the same time when you are running a business:

The Entrepreneur - The entrepreneur represents the visionary and creative element within us. He/she sees the 'future' and is filled with enthusiasm about building something big, something of his/her own.

The Manager - The manager represents the pragmatic element. He is concerned with facts, statistics, planning, order, and management. Where the entrepreneur might see an opportunity, the manager sees a problem.

The Technician - This is the element that does the actual work.

The technician does not care about 'ideas', he cares about 'how to do the things.'

'The Entrepreneur lives in the future, and The Manager lives in the past. The Technician lives in the present.'

Surprisingly, these three roles within us are in constant battle with each other - the entrepreneur is always starting new projects for the managers and technicians to carry out; the manager is trying to put everything into a 'system' or 'a way of doing things,' and the technician does the work as well as he can.

Ultimately, the imbalance among these three elements of the personality lead to a failed business. Most businesses start with only one personality aspect - the technician. For example, a web developer starts a web-development agency. A plumber begins a plumbing service company. A graphic designer starts a design shop.

According to Michael Gerber, from his conversations with hundreds of small business owners, "The typical small business owner is only 10 percent Entrepreneur, 20 percent Manager, and 70 percent Technician."

The motivation that drives a technician to start his own company is that he doesn't want to work for a boss. He understands the technical work, so he wants to work for himself. However, he fails to imagine that a business requires numerous types of work besides the technical work itself. Ironically, he ends up being a more miserable boss than the one he left. So, this is why most small business don't get sold: they aren't saleable. In order to build a business that you can sell, you need to see your business from a completely different perspective; as Gerber names it, "the turn-key revolution." The turn-key revolution is a concept through which you can transform a business from chaos and disorder into a process that ensures order, excitement, and continuous growth.

Gerber uses the history of McDonald's as the perfect outcome of the turn-key revolution; its offspring is the business format franchise model. Unlike 'trade name' franchises, where only the trade or brand name is franchised, a business format franchise lends its brand name as well as an entire format for doing business. The turn-key revolution and business format franchise go hand-in-hand and they work contrary to this popular belief among entrepreneurs, 'the success of a business resides in the success of the product it sells.' In reality, the true product of a business isn't the product it sells, but rather in how it sells it to the customers.

Studies conducted by the U.S. Commerce Department from 1971 to 1987 report that, yearly, fewer than 5 percent of franchises had been forced out of business, or, over a five-year period, 25 percent. On the other hand, independently-owned businesses were obliged to shut down their operations at a staggering rate of 80 percent over the same five-year period. This clearly indicates the power of the Turn-Key Revolution and the contribution that the Business Format Franchise model makes to the small business arena.

Sell the business, not the product

Even though your business is not a franchise, you need to build your business to the stage where the systems and processes could be packaged up and sold to multiple clients as a franchise. According to Gerber, you need to build a system-dependent business, not a people-dependent business. You need to reengineer all the components of your business so that it can run without YOU.

"Pretend that the business you own is the prototype for 5,000 more like it." Imagine that you are going to franchise your business.

What if you're on a holiday or get sick? What if you have a mental breakdown? If you are unable to free yourself from your business, each time you go away, you will start losing money. Furthermore, you will never be able to sell your business if it is overly dependent on you. So, you need to work ON your business, not IN your business. (You may have heard this phrase numerous times from your local business coach - 'The E-Myth' is the original source!)

Ray Kroc, who took over from the founders of McDonald's, did it perfectly. He worked on McDonald's, not in McDonald's. He introduced the business format franchise model. He wanted to build something that would run without him and would deliver the same results each time, and predictably.

The McDonald brothers thought about their first restaurant just like Henry Ford thought about the Model T. Ray Kroc himself was able to multiply this system throughout the world by offering franchises (watch the movie, 'The Founder'.) He constructed the components of McDonald's so that the entire business system could be replicated over and over again – each one is working and delivering in the same way as the hundreds or thousands that preceded them.

With this model, within forty years, Ray Kroc's McDonald's had become a $40-billion-a-year business, with 28,707 restaurants worldwide, serving food to more than 43 million people every day in 120 countries. They represent more than 10 percent of the gross restaurant receipts in America! You can emulate the same formula for your business, too.

The entrepreneur's job is to create systems, which the manager oversees, and the technician executes.

Continuous and never-ending improvement
When you transform your business into a system of systems, it starts working without you. The system runs the show, and the people run the system. If you've designed the system well, all that is left for other people is to learn about how to run the system. This is what has been done at McDonald's, and at Disney World as well as at Federal Express, including any other extraordinarily successful business you name! These extraordinary businesses draw extraordinary business valuations. Once again, the most successful sellers see their business through the eyes of a buyer. Do not forget that the investor is looking for a cash-flow machine. Imagine his delight in discovering that your company represents a well-oiled cash-flow machine, which operates and grows without its shareholder. Are you already ISO 9001 certified? For my own company, becoming certified

was a way of leaving the business to run by itself. The principles underlying the ISO 9001 are those invented by Deming for Japan's industrial renaissance in the 1950s. If I were to summarise in a phrase what Deming brought to the field of management studies, it would be "continuous and never-ending improvement." When you ask a consultant to set up an ISO 9001 for you, he will set you up providing you with mountains of forms to fill in, procedures to be carried out, and organigrams to study. However, if you manage to prove to your auditor that you are a continuously improving firm, increasing the quality of your products or services on a daily basis, you can do away with most of this paperwork. That is indeed in the spirit of an ISO 9001.

Your buyer will be able to understand how your company works by reviewing your written processes and checklists, and this will give him confidence that your products or services are always provided at the same level of quality, over and over again. He will be buying a system, not a group of people in an industrial unit messing around with Post-It notes but rather a true cash-flow machine.

DO YOU FOLLOW A "SUPEROWNER" MODEL?

If you were to draw a sketch that represents your role in your company, what would it look like? Are you at the top end of a traditional org chart, or are you stuck in the middle of your business, like the hub of a bicycle wheel?

As anyone who has tried to fly British Airways when Heathrow has been hit by a storm knows, a hub-and-spoke model is only as strong as the hub. The moment the hub is under pressure, the entire system goes wrong. Acquirers generally avoid Superowner-managed businesses because they understand the dangers of buying a company too dependent on the owner. Here's a list of clues you're a Superowner and some suggestions for pulling yourself out of the middle of your business:

1. Do you sign all the cheques or control the bank transfers?

Most business owners sign the cheques, but what happens if you're away for a couple of days and an important supplier needs to be paid? Consider giving an employee signing authority for cheques or for validating bank transfers up to an amount you're comfortable with and mandate another employee to review the bank statements. This gives your business a "checks and balances" system to make sure the privileges aren't abused. Think of the Sovereign and the Prime Minister who have influence over each other. In theory, none can exceed their constitutional duties, because they each have a degree of oversight with regard to the other.

2. Is your mobile phone bill over £200 a month?

If your employees are out of their depth a lot, it will show up in your mobile phone bill because you will be calling staff regularly to steer them through problems. Ask yourself whether you're hiring too many junior employees. Sometimes people with a couple of years of industry experience will be a lot more self-sufficient and only slightly more expensive than juniors. Also consider getting a virtual assistant (VA), or a personal assistant, who can act as a protector of your time and schedule.

3. Is your turnover flat when compared to last year's?

Flat turnover from one year to the next can be a sign you are a hub in a hub-and-spoke model. No matter how good you are, if your business is too dependent on you, it will start to plateau. Consider removing from your product or service range the offers which are so complex they require your personal involvement.

4. Are your holidays disappointing for your family?

If you spend your holidays giving orders to others on your mobile phone, reducing your family time, it's time to break free, or rather to let your employees break free. Could you start by taking one day off and seeing how your company does without you? Buyers will love your company if you work up to a point where you can take a few weeks off without your business suffering. Sometimes businesses actually benefit from the absence of their overbearing owner!

5. Do you spend a lot of time negotiating?

If you find yourself constantly involved in approving discount requests or special deals from your customers, you are in the way of normal business operations. Consider giving front-line, customer-facing employees a range within which they may negotiate and enticing them never to give a discount for free, but always to ask for something in return, like faster payment. You may also want to link your sales team's bonus to gross margin in order to reward their contribution to profit, rather than turnover.

6. Do you close the "shop" every night?

If you are in charge of the close-up process (set the alarm, lock the doors, count the cash), then you are in the way. Start drafting a manual of standard operating procedures and give it to new staff on their first day on the job. For guidance on this, I recommend reading "Work the System", by Sam Carpenter.

7. Do you know all your clients personally?

It's good to have great relationships with clients, but not so good if you are the only one having them. Relying too heavily on your personal relationships you might see as the glue that holds your business together. Replace yourself as a key sales person by hiring a sales team, and have a trusted employee join you when you meet customers so that over time, they build relationships with someone else.

8. Do your suppliers invite you to rugby matches?

Suppliers trying to gain your good favours by sending you tickets to events can be a sign that they see you as the key decision-maker in your business. If you indeed are, you will find yourself in the hub of your business when it comes time to negotiating terms. Consider appointing one of your trusted employees as the key contact for a major supplier and give that employee spending authority up to a limit that you're comfortable with. The next step is to make the procurement process more scientific, like in major companies, where purchasing is a KPI-led process rather than a relationship one.

9. Are you deluged with emails?

Staff, clients, and suppliers constantly copying you in on e-mails can be a sign that they are looking for your implicit approval or that you have not clarified at which stage, if any, you want to be involved in their processes. Start by asking your employees to stop using the copy line in an e-mail; ask them to add you to the "to" line if you really must take a decision or carry out a specific action on something.

Focus on profits

In the UK, as in most of the OECD countries, it is not tax efficient to draw large salaries. Since the recent dividend tax changes, it is only slightly more tax efficient to derive one's income from dividends. Accountants throughout the country usually recommend to owner operators a mixture of income in the form of salary and dividends, typically equating to c. £40K for a single shareholder, or 80K for a married shareholder couple. This has conscious and unconscious consequences on the profits of most SMEs.

Let me explain: if you know it will not be tax efficient to generate more than about £70K of net profit, then you are not going to try very hard to maximise your net profit. Imagine the case where the tax brackets allowed business owners to pay themselves £100K each with very little tax. As a consequence, you could be sure that the typical net profit in SMEs would be close to the £100K for a single shareholder, or to the £200K mark for a couple of shareholders. The tax system is designed to encourage a specific behaviour. As you can see, it also has unexpected consequences on the profits declared by the SMEs. If it is not tax efficient to earn more than £50K in net profit, then it will be all the more tempting to finance the owner's lifestyle through deductible expenses, like a company car, a new iPad, or a business/holiday trip.

Hence profits are limited to what the owner needs, but the businesses though are not managed to maximize profits. I suggest you get into a profit mindset as this is what the buyer will be motivated by, not your company car, nor your company-sponsored club membership. I recommend reading "Profit First", a book by Mike Michalowicz. This book reminded me, as a business owner of the real reasons we are all in business: to make and maximise profit.

Have good financial controls in place

You need to start thinking about ways to maximise profitability before deciding to sell your business. Starting these initiatives in the middle of a sale process means you have missed your best opportunity to enhance value. Ideally, you want to have demonstrable and higher earnings over 3 years by the time you want to sell. Focus on achieving those operational efficiencies, cost reductions, and other value-enhancers in advance, so that hey can be easily and indubitably demonstrated.

Having a financial controller or finance director in place is a good start to implementing strong financial controls. Take time to really understand your business operations and look at profitability from an objective standpoint. Reliable financial statements, and accurate, timely reporting are attractive features that often influence a buyer's decision. Presenting your business as one that generates solid cash flows with a strong management team, as well as lower capital expenditure requirements, will position it as an attractive acquisition.

To most buyers you are selling future cash flows. Make sure you have a realistic and supportable forecast to show. This points to the credibility of management and the quality of the business. Providing potential buyers with forecasts that are reasonable, believable, and achievable (with some degree of specificity or detail) can further demonstrate the underlying value of a business. Generally appropriate for cash-generating, mature, stable businesses, and those with good long-term prospects, this more technical method depends heavily on the assumptions made about long-term business conditions. Essentially, the valuation of your business will always, in the end, be based on multiples of profits. A great tool to have in your business is a 3-month, or 1-year, cash- flow forecast. Cash is the blood of your small business. Having a forecast will enable you to focus on the generation of cash, rather than on the accounting profits of your business.

Also, keep in mind that your business has to appeal to the lender who will be financing your buyer. The more your company's cash flow is predictable and secure, the higher the likelihood the lender will accept to share the risk with the buyer.

INTERVIEW

KEVIN ANSETT

Director, Pecunia (2016) Limited

Kevin helps businesses improve their cashflow

Maidstone

www.pecunia2016.co.uk

What are the benefits of having a well-managed cash flow?

The main benefit of good cash flow is that it helps you deal with fundamental expenses: rent, staff, suppliers. Good cash flow can also boost your credit rating which can then lead to better access to credit, which certainly gives the business peace of mind. Good cash flow keeps the business operating, leading to stability and the potential to grow.

It also allows for any unforeseen events that come up and may need some cash injection or cash funding. Getting a good reputation in the marketplace by paying all your bills on time helps tremendously. An added benefit of this is that a business will have better access to finance as well as potentially growing the business through acquisition.

How are credit scores for businesses calculated?

Credit-scoring agencies base themselves on the financial statements. They look at the level of cash, the current ratio (current assets/current liabilities), the quick ratio (current assets − inventory)/current liabilities, the debt to equity ratio, as well as the payment history insofar it is reported to the agency.

In addition, the agency will consider anything in the public domain, such as county court judgments. Businesses which are fond of paying bills by credit card that may leave a footprint which may have a slightly negative rating. If the business is a sole trader or a partnership, a lot of its financial scoring will be based on the individual's financial capacity.

When you speak to your clients, which key steps do you advise to improve cash flow?

First of all, businesses that do credit checks before accepting a client are 30% less likely to fail. Secondly, a business needs to ensure it has robust terms and conditions, including clear payment terms. We advocate that every business, no matter how small or large, should have a credit policy to which everybody in the organisation adheres. This policy should state that a new client account should always be signed off by the credit manager. Once trading starts, the credit manager needs to stay involved to make sure the client is behaving well.

A business should have a sound credit-control function, making sure that there are policies in place for sending out invoices on time, as all invoices should be sent out within 24 hours of the job being done. I still see small businesses that do the job on the first of the month but do not invoice until the 30th of the month! That has a terrible impact on the cash flow. There also needs to be a process for when the account is overdue, which entails calling the customer as quickly as possible. For larger customers, it is preferable to phone beforehand, and have a proactive collection technique. Thereafter, make sure you follow up with a polite reminder by post. Make sure that you do not threaten the customer if you have no intentions of following through.

A good credit controller is a confident operative, who knows the job and speaks regularly to customers on the telephone. Pick someone who's not frightened to pick up the phone! Don't be afraid to ask for payment: all you're asking for is part of the sales contract. As you fulfilled your obligations, it is now the customer's turn to fulfil theirs by paying the invoice.

How do you recommend that businesses keep an eye on their cash flow?

Any form of cash flow forecast is a really good way to start. There are some simple templates which smaller businesses can pick up on the internet. It will focus the company on what exactly is coming in to the company and what is going out each month. Sometimes, when business owners are very focused on their skills, their unique products and services, they may forget about cash flow. Some business owners still don't understand the difference between profits and cash flow, thinking all is fine if the company is making a profit. However, cash is needed in the business to pay wages, suppliers, and so on.

Even profitable companies have gone down by running out of cash. Again, you need robust and proactive monitoring of all cash inflows and outflows, highlighting and acting on late payments so that you can still meet the financial commitments of your business.

Do you think it's easier to sell the company with a good cash flow and credit control systems?

An investor, a lender, or a trade buyer will certainly look at the profits, the products, etc. But unless you've got a first-class credit control function, and you have cash in the business, then I know from first-hand experience that the deal will fail. Lenders will be concerned by the overdue invoices, and will be wary of taking on the personal guarantee for the overdraft. I advocate a good credit control function is paramount to any business that is looking for a buyer.

CHARACTERISTICS THAT MAKE YOUR COMPANY MORE VALUABLE THAN YOUR COMPETITORS

The value of your company is partly determined by your sector. For example, cloud-based software companies are generally worth more than haulage companies these days. However, even when analysing business sales in the same industry, there are major variations in valuation.

1. Recurring turnover

The more the turnover originates from monthly recurring contracts or subscriptions, the more valuable your business will be to a buyer. Even if subscriptions are not the norm in your sector, if you can find some form of recurring turnover (in the form of maintenance contracts, for instance), it will increase your company's desirability.

2. Niche positioning

Trade buyers, in particular, buy what they cannot easily replicate on their own. Private investors are reassured by a "blue ocean" marketplace. Hence, companies with a unique product or service that is difficult for a competitor to copy are more valuable than a business that sells a commodity. If your company does sell a commodity, think about your Unique Selling Proposition. What makes the customer choose you above any other option in the marketplace, including doing nothing?

3. Growth

Trade buyers looking to increase sales growth through acquisition will pay a premium for your company if it is growing much faster than its sector peers.

4. Trendy

Tired old trade buyers often try to buy excitement through the acquisition of a trendy young business in their sector. If you are the jewel of your sector's trade publication, expect to get a premium acquisition offer.

5. Emplacement

If you have a great location with natural physical characteristics that are difficult to replicate (think of a freight forwarder right next to the port of Dover), you'll have buyers who understand that your business, like a medieval castle, is surrounded by an anti-competition "moat".

6. Diverse customer list

Buyers pay a premium, or at least don't discount the price of a company which has little customer concentration. Make sure no customer amounts to more than 5 percent of your turnover, and your company will be more valuable than a competitor's that has just a few big customers. Plus, you can tell your disrespectful and late-paying clients to go fly a kite on Camber Sands!

7. Processed sales and marketing

If you have developed a sales and marketing process, with a documented conversion rate, and a conversion funnel to go with it, your secret customer-acquiring formula will make your company more valuable to an acquirer than a competitor who is counting on word of mouth to get his next client.

8. Good books and records

Businesses that invest in audited statements have financials that are usually viewed by acquirers as more trustworthy. You may want to get your books reviewed professionally each year even if audited statements are not necessary for your size of business. In any case, make sure that you have at least 3 years of clean books and records, which can be easily audited by the buyer's due diligence team. It goes without saying but avoid any off-the-books cash movements. It's illegal, unfair, and the buyer won't be able to take it into account in their valuation.

9. A second- level management

Businesses with second-level management, having agreed to remain with the company after the sale, is more valuable than businesses where all the power and knowledge are in the hands of the owner. In addition, the lender won't commit funds without the incumbent management staying on, or at least without a clear succession plan, shouldered by the current MD.

10. Happy clients

Being able to prove that your clients are happy and intend to keep on buying from you will make your business more valuable than a competitor's which does not have a means of tracking customer satisfaction.

As when a flowing tide lifts all boats, your broad sector typically defines a range of multiples within which your business is likely to sell for. However, whether you are at the bottom or at the top of the range comes down to elements that have nothing to do with your sector, but rather on, how you run your business.

Accumulate retained earnings

As previously stated, most OECD members, including the UK, have different levels of tax according to the type of income concerned. Salary income is the most highly taxed: income tax's marginal tax rate after £150K of income is high (the additional rate is as high as 46%). Dividend income comes next.

Capital gains tax is usually the lowest of tax rates; in the UK, the CGT is at 20%, or 28% for residential property. Yet, we are privileged to have a lower regime of capital gains tax called, Entrepreneurs Relief. Business owners who sell their shares, or sole traders who sell their assets, and who meet the criteria of Entrepreneurs Relief only pay 10% of Capital Gains Tax. This is one of the lowest of all the OECD economies, on a par with Luxembourg and Turkey. To qualify for Entrepreneurs Relief, you have to have held the shares for a minimum of 2 years; have to be an employee or an office holder of the company, and the business needs to be a trading activity rather than an investment activity (such as, buy-to-let property, for instance, although holiday rentals do qualify.) Make sure you do not get this wrong! To be certain that you can claim Entrepreneurs Relief go through the criteria with an expert and verify that all the criteria are in place. A common oversight is, for example, the fact that your wife draws dividends from the company but is neither a director nor an employee. In such a case, she would not be eligible for Entrepreneurs Relief, and would have to pay 20% CGT on the sale of her shares. Twenty percent is quite low. Nevertheless, why pay more tax than you have to?

Finally, Entrepreneurs Relief is subjected to a lifetime ceiling of £1m. So, if you own your business with your wife, and you sell your business for £1m, you will both have the capacity to benefit from Entrepreneurs Relief in the future on the next £1m of capital gains.

Frequently, business owners spend the last years of their career accumulating cash. The advice they typically receive from their accountant is to do so in order to extract surplus cash from their business at completion and extract it at the

Entrepreneurs Relief rate of 10% rather than at the marginal tax rate of 46%. However, keep in mind that this cash must have been generated from trading, and must not have been invested. Therefore, do not have the company buy investment property with the surplus cash, and make sure it is not even put in a deposit interest-bearing account. Take great care!

Tell your management team
Selling the business that you founded is a highly emotional exercise. For the first time, you will be opening your books to non-accountant third parties; you will be scrutinised; your decisions evaluated, or even questioned, and your strategic decisions analysed. You might feel occasionally on the defensive, or even angry at the questions thrown your way. In order to avoid this, some business owners ask their management team to manage the process for them. Although they also have an emotional attachment to the company, it is not their company, and they can stand back and view the process in a more dispassionate way.

MIKE

(Wishes to remain anonymous for this interview)

Whitstable

Mike recently sold his company, and asked his management team to orchestrate the disposal process.

What were the advantages of having the management team deal with the sale process?

First, you need to trust your management team enough to share with them your intention to sell and your timing. Before selling the business to a trade buyer, I had worked with my management on raising equity. Therefore, the management team was already aware of this process, and I just had to pivot them towards selling the whole business. The sale process was much easier because our interests were aligned. Since the buyer knew the management team was effectively running the company, they didn't have to ask me to stay after the sale.

Were these managers also shareholders in your business?

Yes. I had sold two of them 5% each, 4 years ago. They got the money from savings, family and friends.

When did you inform your staff?
The staff was informed very late, only a few days before completion.

What would you have done differently, if you could do the process once again?
I would probably have had a stronger shareholder agreement drafted. As it was not written for this purpose, it was a bit weak in the context of this deal. Therefore, I would probably spend more time on it. If you have multiple shareholders in your business, a strong shareholder agreement is probably the most important document for a successful exit. In addition, I think selling shares to management benefited the growth of the company. When you strongly believe you have the right people, it's a good idea to get them onboard and invested in the business.

Although your management team is undoubtedly good at managing your business, selling a company may be very new to them. You could ask a business coach to accompany them during the process, ideally one who has already been through the process of company disposal (quite a few former business owners, having adverse reactions to the concept of retirement, become business coaches.) They could also be given help by the corporate finance adviser you mandate, should you decide to do so.

Tell your employees
Your employees are the working life force of your business. Deciding the best time to tell them is a critical aspect of the acquisition process. To ensure a seamless transition of ownership, it is important to ensure your employees are

as relaxed as possible about the acquisition process. Uncertainty breeds doubt and fear. Therefore, I recommend that you only tell your employees as late as possible to avoid creating a climate of uncertainty which might affect business operations at a delicate point in the transition process. A good time could be after a letter of intent has been signed. This would be at a time when a qualified buyer has been selected, sworn to secrecy, and you have a good chance of getting the deal consolidated with this investor.

However, when you are ready to communicate, go all in. Organise entire staff meetings; if possible, meet each individual staff member separately, and repeat the message over and over again: "I have found a safe pair of hands to take care of the company's future. Our legacy, name, staff and link to the community will be preserved. I have full confidence in the buyer and wish him all the best." Emphasize the positive aspects of the process. You can explain that the company needs new energy and new ideas to move forward and, as you have been in the company for some time, you can no longer see the wood for the trees.

When you make commitments, stick to them. The type of buyer you will select will have a great deal of importance in your staff's eyes. For instance, if you were to sell to a trade buyer, synergies would typically be sought by relocating; making staff cuts to get rid of duplicate roles; changing the name above the door, etc. If you have decided not to sell to a competitor, stick to it. If you commit to sell your business to your employees, keep your promise.

CHAPTER THREE

MAKE YOURSELF READY FOR SALE

Your mindset

So, you have been coming to the office every day, rain or shine, for years and years, and suddenly this will stop. Not brutally of course, but progressively, you won't be needed anymore by the buyer. Can you imagine how that will feel? Demographic studies show a sharp jump in mortality after retirement. The lack of mental stimulation as well as the lack of a certain amount of good stress are considered to be the main causes of early death.

What will you do with your spare time? You may want to spend more time with your family, with your friends, or even start or acquire a new business. Whatever you do, plan it carefully to make sure your brain stays busy and alert and your calendar full in order to avoid depression and idleness.

Buyers and their lenders very often insist that the seller stays on for one or two years after the sale. This may even, in some cases, condition the payment of an earn-out, which is a form of deferred consideration based on financial targets. Staying on will provide the seller with a smooth transition; will reassure the lender and will also give you a gradual way out.

However, many business owners report that their new position as an employee or consultant can be a bit awkward, with confusion arising in the minds of the employees as to who is the boss.

Your age

Your age has a big impact on your attitude toward your company, and your feelings about the perspective of selling it.

For example, one firm of corporate finance advisers refuses to take mandates from business owners over the age of 70. They have found that septuagenarians are so personally invested that they can rarely bring themselves to sell their business - frequently calling off the sale at the eleventh hour, claiming they wouldn't know what to do with themselves if they didn't have a business to run anymore. While it's always dangerous to make generalisations - especially based on something as sensitive as age – a few patterns can emerge.

Owners aged 25 to 49

Business owners in their twenties and thirties nowadays see their businesses as a means to an end, and most expect to sell in the next 5 to 10 years. In a similar manner to their employed class or university friends, who move to a new job every 3 to 5 years, these owners may expect to use the proceeds of their business sale to start or acquire a new business.

Aged 50 to 69

In the post-war years, an employee agreed to be loyal to the company, and, in return, the company agreed to provide a good living and a pension for a few happy years. Many of the business owners in this generation think of their company as more than a source of profit. They see their company as part of a community and, by extension, themselves as community leaders. To many of this generation, the idea of selling their business feels like abandoning their employees and their community. That's why so many business owners in their 50s and 60s know they need to sell to guarantee their company's and their own future, but they want to make sure their loyal employees and their legacy are protected.

Seventy plus
Business owners in their seventies and eighties feel a great sense of loss without their business - that's why so many refuse to sell or experience depression after they do. As a result, many businesses owned by more senior owners run the risk of disappearing along with their founder.

Your finances

What will be your source of cash flow post-sale? You could invest the proceeds in another less risky asset: property, public stocks, bonds.

In terms of personal finance, you will be replacing a source of cash flow by capital. My 4-year-old son said to me when I mentioned I was selling my company, "But daddy, what about your cash flow?"

Although your capital will be more lightly taxed than your salary and dividends, it will also be a one-off. Moreover, if you want to preserve the capital and receive an income from it, it may be difficult to find an investment with a return on investment comparable to that of a small business. Let us say, for example, that you were getting a cash flow of £200K in salary and dividends from your business, which you then sell for £700K. That is a return on equity of 28%. You will be hard pressed to find a replacement asset to acquire with such a return on equity. Since the risk is so much lower, the returns you will be getting in property, or on quoted shares, are closer to the 5% mark. The dividend yield for BP PLC shares is currently 6,11%. Therefore, if you invest your £700K in BP shares, you will only receive £42K of dividend income, which you will not be able to tax optimise using the mixture of salary and dividends which you had in your limited company.

You could also remain as a consultant and invoice your hours; this will be welcomed by the seller and by his lender. However, it may not be a long-term agreement, depending on how much the seller needs you going forward, and how much the business depends on you.

You could also receive the consideration on a deferred basis. For instance, if you agree on a price for your business of £240K, the seller could make 60 monthly payments of £4K to you. If you agree to a deferred consideration, you can also negotiate a higher total value with the seller, which he will likely accept as he will be saving on the lender's interest and minimising his own risk.

You could decide that your other sources of cash flow, such as your pension, suffice, and spend your capital. To be honest, I like this idea. After having worked extremely hard all one's life, a business owner deserves to splash out on some amazing holidays, travel, or even toys for grandchildren. If you have more than enough, go ahead, treat the family and your friends, and enjoy travelling around the world.

Typically, when you sell your small business, you won't get a cheque for the full consideration and ride away into the sunset. Most of the time, you will receive a mixture of initial payment and a deferred consideration. You could also agree with the buyer, should it make more sense to you, to receive the entire consideration on a deferred basis, paid monthly, quarterly, or annually. This is particularly useful when the particularities of your business make it difficult for the seller to get a loan to finance the acquisition. You could also negotiate, in exchange for a deferred consideration, a higher total value for your shares.

The initial consideration could be anything from 10% to 100% of the total consideration. Before you accept the level of down payment, do keep in mind that in order to claim Entrepreneurs Relief, you will have to declare the whole amount of your capital gains in your next self-assessment, which means that you will also have to pay your tax before 31 January of the following tax year. For example, if you sell your company on 15 February 2021, you will declare it in your self-assessment for the 2020-2021 tax year and will have to pay it before the 31st of January 2022. Make sure that the initial consideration is enough to cover your tax bill, i.e. at least 10% of the total consideration.

CHAPTER FOUR

BE WELL ADVISED

Do you need an advis er?

Do you fix your teeth yourself? The answer is no, since you go to a dentist. It is always useful to use a specialist who does one thing year in, year out, and does it well. You don't want to risk what is typically your most valuable asset based on bad advice. Reading this book is a good start (you will save a lot of money if you follow the recommendations on how to claim Entrepreneurs Relief or how to extract surplus cash, for instance). However, it is of great benefit to be guided by a professional.

Which advisers do you need?

A business broker - The broker will manage the sale process:

- Advise on the price;
- Prepare a data room;
- Prepare an IM;
- Advertise the business;
- Receive the offers;
- Check the buyers' credentials and source of funds;
- Prepare the LOI;
- Apply pressure on the advisers to execute the deal.

A corporate finance adviser, or M&A adviser, is basically a more prestigious way to label a business broker. The business brokerage market is not regulated and, hence, anyone can call himself a business broker. However, corporate finance advisers are typically authorised by the FCA or registered with the Institute of Chartered Accountants. Understanding the standard pricing structure brokers adopt can be a major cost-saver and your knowledge of these structures will also save you some unwanted terms when trying to sell your business. Clinton Lee, founder of the EXIT firm (ukbusinessbrokers.com), notes that employing a business broker will usually cost you around 8%-10% of the total business listing or selling price, with exceptional cases going as low as 1.5%, and 12% on the high-end. However, fee structure varies widely depending on factors like size and a broker's mode of operation.

According to Clinton, you can differentiate between brokers by considering the way they charge fees. The largest brokers implement aggressive client acquisition models, using large-scale cold calling, and will typically charge a percentage after successfully selling your business. This no-sale-no-fee model is the reason why most businesses listed for sale in the UK are represented by such brokers. You simply need to sign the contract and they will market your business for you, but you should be wary of the terms included in such agreements.

The other class of brokers primarily targets larger businesses. They charge a retainer fee for the work that needs to be done prior to the business going on the market. The larger the business, the higher the fee, so a business with a revenue of £50 million will incur a higher retainer fee than a business with a turnover of between £1 million and £10 million.

Business brokers who may already have contacted you include such firms as BCMS, KBS Corporate, Avondale, or Evolution CBS. There are many firms in this market, and it can be a bit confusing. If you want to mandate a broker, I recommend you speak to Clinton as he is the expert in selecting the right broker for the right business.

Most sellers I spoke to are quite disappointed with their broker for one of the following reasons:

- They don't do much beyond advertising it for sale;
- The IM is a bit light or of a "boilerplate" type;
- They are slow to reply to your information request and are slow in managing investor inquiries;
- Most of all, the offers you will receive for the company are typically much lower than the valuation provided to you in the first place. Brokers do tend to give inflated valuations to businessowners to flatter them, get them dreaming so that they sign the contract. Disappointment comes at a later stage for the seller;
- If you work on a success-fee basis with your broker, your interests may not be aligned. The broker wants to sell your business to be able to focus their resources on the next deal. To him/her, a £100K increase in the sale price will only mean an £5K additional fee. Can you see the asymmetric incentive to get a better deal from the buyer?

Corporate finance advisers

If you want more personalised advice, it may be a good option to consider using the services of a corporate finance adviser. It is wise to pay your adviser a retainer in addition to a success fee in order to make sure that your interests are aligned.

Your corporate finance adviser can be locally based, which will allow him to reach out to local private investors, family offices, or private equity firms.

You can also mandate a sector-specific corporate finance adviser, who knows your industry and who the likely trade buyers are.

Many business owners looking to exit inform their accountant. The company's accountant is not necessarily a good source of advice on the disposal process, as it is quite a specialist field. It can also be tempting to listen to one's accountant to get a valuation. However, if you don't want to end up with an unrealistic idea of the value of your business, it is better to speak to a specialist. Your chartered accountant can however be of help in order to make your company's accounts as attractive as possible for a buyer. He will advise you on how to maximise profits, account for depreciation or compile the financial data room which will satisfy the buyer as well as the lender's due diligence team.

You will save a lot of time and money by selecting a corporate finance lawyer. Although it may be tempting to ask your family lawyer, your golf buddy lawyer, or your generalist business lawyer to represent you, you will save time by selecting your local legal corporate finance expert. You need a dealmaker who gets deals done, not a deal killer, who just wants to preserve the existing relationship with your company or to justify their fees.

Although all these advisers are corporate finance specialists, you also need to take responsibility if the deal stalls. Sometimes also, it helps to get the advisers out of the way, to lock yourself in a meeting room with the buyer, and to work out the disagreements. I believe all business owners should have a business coach. The main purpose of a coach is to hold you accountable to the vision and the goals you define. Your coach will gently remind you of your commitments, and make sure you get things done. A business coach will also be there to assist you during the disposal process, and make sure you have a clear vision of what value you want for your business.

Don't hide behind your advisers. The key success factor in a deal is rapport building between the seller and the buyer. If the buyer can't speak to you face to face without half a dozen advisers being there as well, or isn't given access to you to build trust and rapport, he may get discouraged and lose interest.

Solicitors

A solicitor will protect your interests throughout the transaction. In particular, the solicitor will make sure that the documents drafted by the buyer's solicitors, i.e. the Heads of Terms and the Sale and Purchase agreement, are in your interest, and will advise you to negotiate better terms if necessary.

It is critical that you retain a highly specialised solicitor, focused on commercial law, and ideally on small business disposals. It is recommended that you negotiate with your solicitor a flat fee for the whole transaction all the way to completion, otherwise your legal bill can run up, especially if you have a picky buyer on the other side, or complex issues, such as the transfer of property assets.

Typical sell-side solicitor fees are in the region of £10K, provided the deal is straightforward and there are not complex legal (especially tax or property), issues to deal with.

Accountants

Your accountant will make sure your books and records are ready for the financial due diligence. He will also advise you on getting your tax affairs in order; are you using a particular scheme which you aren't very proud of? The accountant will get rid of that for you, to make sure your business is as clean as possible.

If you own property in the business, your accountant will also probably advise you to lodge it in a separate holding company or pension fund, which will then charge rent to your business. Most business investors I know don't want to acquire property: they are interested in the business.

Be wary of asking your accountant for a valuation; unless the firm has a corporate finance arm, valuing companies and listening to the M&A market isn't something accountants do. Many sellers have unrealistic valuations based on their accountants advice. Speak to a corporate finance adviser instead.

CHAPTER FIVE

DIFFERENT TYPES OF BUYERS

Your children

Your business will be considered a family business if you pass it on to the next generation. Building a family business is a great way to preserve your legacy through the generations and to share a unique opportunity with your children. Handing your business over to the next generation does not mean gifting it, although the UK has quite a generous tax regime for share gifts. For inheritance tax purposes, a gift of shares to your child is called a lifetime transfer. If you survive 7 years after the gift, there is no inheritance tax to pay.

We usually are quite aware of our children's financial situation and tend to believe they could not acquire our business due to lack of financial means. Nothing is further from the truth. If your children are strongly motivated to take over your business as the next family generation in charge, many options exist. If there is a difficulty with raising the initial consideration, the easiest way to organise the transition is to offer that your child pay the value of the business on a 100% deferred basis. That way, the consideration can be paid out of the dividends of the company, monthly or yearly, whichever suits you best.

If you require an initial consideration and if there is not enough surplus cash in the company to provide you with one, you can team your child up with an investor (like me) who can take a share of the equity and can also take an advisory seat on the board.

INTERVIEW

ANITA BRIGHTLEY-HODGES

Chairman, Family Business Place

Anita helps family businesses with succession planning

Maidstone

www.familybusinessplace.com

Should you gift your company to your children or sell it to them?

If you plan to gift your shares, as an advisor I would ask the children if they were prepared to buy the shares from their family. If they respond affirmatively, then I'd know they are ready for the challenge. If they don't, I would recommend that you all think again about it.

There are 4 reasons why you would join the family business. One is because you are passionate about it. Second, if you didn't join, then your family business would cease to exist, and it is often the case that the family name is above the door. The third is, if you would be depriving the family of its income, which it may depend on. And the fourth reason is that you can't get a job from anywhere else. At least if know where your children stand on these options, you can act accordingly and put the appropriate training and development in place.

As the business owner, you really have to understand what your children's aspirations are; what they want, and how they would get on with each other. Also, do not forget consulting their most trusted advisor, too - their wife or husband.

In which generation are family businesses most at risk?

The third generation is the most difficult one. There is a well-known phrase:

shirtsleeves to shirtsleeves: the first generation starts the business, the second generation builds it, and the third generation may very well squander it. Family businesses are renowned for succession by meritocracy, as in a non-family business, and are often accused of nepotism. Research shows only 30% of businesses successfully transition generation 1 to 2; only 12% from generation 2 to 3, and only 4% survive from generation three onwards.

The high failure rate is mainly understood because of two essential factors - poor communication between family members, and failure to plan the future adequately and in a timely way. Planning is essential; it can be planning for an exit, for a sale, for succession, a merger, planning for growth via employee ownership or franchise. Most family businesses don't really understand that they have options, and the impact their choice will have on both the business and the wider family.

Typically, are children still interested in carrying on the family business as before?

Many parents would rather the children do their own thing: go to university, travel the world, go to work for somebody else first and get some extra skills before coming back and working in the family business. Children with an exposure to the wider world are less at risk from frustration and the feeling that they have not chosen their career with the passion that drives us. Many children can be interested in carrying the family business on if they feel that they are doing something they love, and that they can own and be responsible for their role in it. The ability to bring their skillset to the family business has to go hand-in-hand with the parents being open to change, for example, by embracing new technology or in seeking new markets. The key selling points if you want to persuade your children to take on the family business are: flexibility, a balanced lifestyle, inclusion in decision making, being accountable, having their ideas listened to, and getting leadership training and development. These are values that millennials appreciate and seek out. They can find these benefits in a family business in a way that corporate employers fail to understand or provide.

The broke buyers

For the past few years there have been quite a few training companies popping up teaching aspiring business buyers to acquire companies without using any of their own money. People who undergo this training are typically existing business owners, or opportunistic-minded entrepreneurs.

These buyers typically have little personal capital but a great deal of motivation and thirst for new knowledge. Although hundreds go through these training programmes every year, only a tiny percentage end up actually buying a business; most get discouraged by their high failure rate, and their lack of success in identifying business owners happy to go along with their suggested deal structures. Two types of deals are usually put forward:

The 100% leveraged model

A leveraged buy out is a transaction where the buyer will look at the company's assets and try to leverage them using a specialist lender or his/her own bank. There is a risk of overleveraging a business by piling on debt it cannot repay. Although most LBOs include a share of equity invested by the buyer, some highly leveraged deals are 100% debt financed – this is possible but is risky.

An asset-backed lender can use several kinds of company assets as collateral: inventory, debtors, or property. Raising asset-backed debt for acquisition finance makes complete sense, and is used all the time. However, as "broke" buyers are dependent on the company assets to raise finance, they will only be able to give you as an initial consideration the amount they can raise against the assets. Moreover, beyond a partial personal guarantee, they will have little "skin in the game": if ever the deal turns sour, they can be tempted to walk away. I recommend always making sure your acquirer injects some of his own funds (personal or corporate) into an acquisition - at least 10% of the initial consideration. This sorts the wheat from the chaff and makes sure your interests are aligned. Moreover, would you sell your business to someone who can't manage their personal finances well enough to save for a downpayment?

The 100% deferred consideration

These buyers will suggest that your business is entirely paid from future profits, in the form of a deferred consideration. Although 100% deferred consideration deals are done from time to time, especially if your company is asset rich and profit poor, if you have a profitable company, with unique strengths, you should be able to get better than that. Once again, make sure your interests are aligned with the seller's by making sure that he has "skin in the game"; typically, in the form of equity contributed to the deal. Beware of 100% deferred deals with zero cash invested by the buyer.

The trade buyers

Trade buyers, aka strategic buyers, can be a great option. They typically can pay more because they will perceive that they can reap the benefits of synergies, which would typically materialise by adding your clients to their list without all your administrative burden. They will often seek to save on administration costs

- by moving your staff to their existing premises, saving on the current lease (not so good if you own the unit);
- by pruning staff which duplicate with existing members of their team;
- by rationalising marketing by getting rid of your brand;
- by integrating their new acquisition into their own company's culture.

These "low hanging fruit" may very well translate in a higher purchase price for your shares, or the assets of the company. Indeed, asset sales are preferred by trade buyers as a form of protection against hidden liabilities.

However, you may have issues with the side effects of a trade sale; typically, the loss of your brand, culture, and legacy, the dismissal of loyal staff members, or the move to a new site in Slough or Peterborough. Be sure to understand the trade buyer's vision, and to make sure their values match yours.

WHICH IS BETTER, A PRIVATE INVESTOR OR A TRADE BUYER?

If you decide to sell your business to an outside buyer, you are going to have to decide between a private investor and a trade buyer - understanding the different perspectives of these two buyers can be a way of getting the best price for your business.

A financial buyer, such as a private investor or private equity firm, is acquiring your future profit stream. To that effect, they will evaluate your company based on how much profit it is likely to make and how reliable that source of profit is likely to be.

But there is a limit to how much they will pay, because financial buyers are limited by the covenants of their lenders. Typically, banks lend a maximum of 2,5x EBITDA. Therefore, the difference between the price you are expecting, be it 3x or 4x EBITDA, must either come from the buyer's equity, or be paid to you on a deferred basis. Financial buyers are opportunistic. They don't have sales teams to sell your product or a network of distributors where your product could be sold. They don't even have to have knowledge of your sector.

They are simply trying to get a return on their investors' money, or on their own money. They will want to get their own equity investment back in 2 or 3 years, maximum. They tend to buy small and mid-sized businesses using a combination of equity, debt, and deferred consideration. Contrary to private investors, who may well hold on for the long term, private equity funds typically have the hope of selling your business five to seven years after the acquisition.

Because financial buyers are usually investors and not operators, they want you and your team to stick around, so they usually defer the payment of a part of the consideration to make sure that you remain involved.

A trade buyer is a different animal - usually a larger company in your sector, they are evaluating your business based on what it is worth in their hands. They will try and estimate how much of their product or service they can sell if they added you to their own range of products and services. Because of their size, this can often lead to buyers who are willing and able to pay much more for your business.

INTERVIEW

BRIAN WEATHERLY
President, International Dental Practice Solutions at a Fortune 500 Company
Faversham

As a strategic buyer, what makes a target business attractive to you?
What we're looking for is alignment with our existing businesses. It could either be a business selling a similar product to what we already provide, or it could be a complementary product to our current offering.

How do you typically structure a deal?
Each deal is unique. But the typical way that we would structure a deal is to require the commitment of the current owner for a given time. Therefore, we would either leave the current owner with shares in their business (up to 49%), depending on the owner's wishes, or offer a deferred consideration over a 2, 3, or 5-year period. In the case of a purchase of a majority ownership of the company, we would typically pay more for the remaining shares in the future.

Does selling to a large corporate always mean the end for the name, the legacy, and the staff of an acquired SME?
It depends. In many cases the acquirer will try to integrate the target business into the larger company. However, in some cases, the brand can live on, and most of the staff can be retained.

Would you have any additional advice from a strategic buyer's perspective for small business owners who want to sell their businesses?

Just try to define, with your family and/or professional advisers, what kind of an exit you want. The price is obviously an important factor, but the legacy of the business is just as much of one. You ask all the important questions and choose the buyer carefully.

The financial buyers

Private equity

If your business is profitable enough to interest PE firms (typically with over £1m in profit before tax), you are likely to be able to get a good valuation, especially if you organise a competitive process. Currently a lot of money lies in the coffers of private equity firms, ready to be invested ("dry powder"), and with more money than deals (or sense). Use that to your advantage.

For smaller firms you can also get financial buyers interested.

Visa investors

Many people want to come and live in the UK, looking for the rule of law, personal safety, and a business-friendly climate. In order to attract foreign capital and entrepreneurs, the UK government has put in place a specific visa allowing a special path to UK residence and citizenship. The Tier 1 Entrepreneur and Investor visas give individuals with respectively £200K and £2m to invest in UK businesses the right to live in the UK.

Private investors

These are private individuals with available liquid capital, typically business owners having recently exited their own company. The typical persona of this kind of buyer has started a company in their 20s or 30s and has exited it in their 40s or 50s. They have a long experience of running a small business, and although financially independent, want to take on a new challenge. Usually business and financially astute, they won't typically overpay for your business, but they will give you a fair market value and have both the capital and the relationships with lenders to make the deal happen.

In addition to private investors, family offices are increasingly interested in small business acquisitions. The source of a family office's funds is family money, typically from the sale or the operation of a larger business.

Your existing management team

You've heard of management buy-outs. As you are an entrepreneur, and like taking your future in your own hands, here is something that should suit you even better: you can organise a VIMBO, a Vendor Initiated Management Buy Out. This situation is ideal as you control the buyers, the price, and the terms, and provide a great opportunity for your worthy management team.

As with a management buy-out, the difficulty is always that the management contributes to the initial consideration. Few employees have the capital required to acquire a valuable asset like a profitable SME. However, that will also be a proof of their motivation in taking on the challenge of owning a small business. You can advise your management that friends as well as family are a good way to find the required capital. They can also team up with a local private investor such as Kent Business Investors.

An Employee Ownership Trust

An EOT sounds like something from 70s Britain, however it is a modern and highly tax efficient way to exit your business. The main advantage is the ability to sell your business, on your terms, to a Trust set up to represent the employees' interest. You can sell your business to the Trust at a fair market price (subject to HMRC approval, but this can reach 6x EBITDA), including any surplus cash. You control the sale process, with low transaction costs and a short deal timeframe. You also retain control during the earn out period. Typically the Trust finances the acquisition, beyond paying surplus cash, by a 100% deferred consideration. A debt-financed transaction is more unusual, but also possible. Last not least, you pay 0% CGT on all proceeds.

Qualifying buyers

You want to avoid wasting time with the people who don't have any capital to acquire your business. This won't be as much of an issue with trade buyers, as they will probably be known to you, and have some financial information publicly available, at least for quoted companies, or UK limited companies. In addition, you can request a copy of their full accounts to observe their cash reserves, cash flow, and profitability. Beware of competitors fishing for information; avoid releasing critical information to a trade buyer before Heads of Terms are signed.

In order to qualify a private buyer, you can simply request a copy of their bank statement; depending on the size of the proposed transaction, make sure they have a commensurate amount available as cash. A few hundred grand in available liquid funds is a credibility booster. These funds can provide enough equity to raise a term loan, or to provide you with a decent down payment in advance of the future payment of a deferred consideration.

CHAPTER SIX

HOW MUCH IS YOUR COMPANY WORTH?

Valuation methods

Your business is likely to be your largest asset, so it's normal to want to know what it is worth. The problem is: business valuation is not so much a science as a market-wide or sector-wide custom.

The science part is what people go to school to learn: you can get university degree in finance, or you can learn the theory behind business valuation. In the UK, there are consulting firms specialising in business valuation.

This book provides the basic rules behind the most common business valuation techniques, but keep in mind that there will always be outliers that fall well outside of these frameworks. In addition, keep in mind the universal rule: a business's value is what it is worth in the acquirer's hands. Strategic acquisitions, however, represent the minority of deals. Here are three valuation methods for your consideration:

Asset-based

The most basic way to value a business is to consider the value of its tangible assets minus its debts, i.e. its Net Asset value. Imagine a haulage company with lorries and trailers. These fixed assets have a value, which can be calculated by estimating the market value of the equipment.

This valuation method often renders the lowest value for your company because it assumes your company does not have any goodwill. According to accountancy principles, goodwill is the difference between the price paid for your company and the value of your net assets.

Typically, companies have at least some goodwill, so in most cases you get a higher valuation by using one of the other two methods described below.

You shouldn't add the results of these valuation techniques. For example, if you are using DCF or comparables, the net assets of the company are assumed to be integral to the generation of the profit and therefore not to be added on to a DCF or Comparables valuation.

A money-losing warehouse sitting on a property with approved residential planning is going to be better off using the Asset-based valuation method; whereas a cleaning company that expects to earn £500,000 next year, but has little in the way of assets, will get a higher valuation using the Discounted Cash Flow method or the comparables technique.

Discounted Cash Flow

In this method, the acquirer is estimating what your future cash flow is worth to them today. They start by forecasting how much free cash flow to equity you expect to make in the next few years.

Once the buyer estimates this, and what your business will be worth when they want to sell it in the future, the buyer will apply a "discount rate" that takes into account the time value of money. The discount rate is determined by the acquirer's cost of capital and how risky they perceive your business to be.

Don't focus too much on the calculations behind the DCF model; it is better to understand the drivers of value when you use this method. They are: 1) how much profit your business is expected to make in the future; and 2) how reliable these estimates are.

In actual fact, few business buyers use the DCF method. M&A departments and analysts of investment banks are usually fond of this technique as it gives them an alternative to the comparables method, and they have the time and resources to conduct the complex financial modelling involved in this method.

Comparables

The most common valuation technique is to look at the value of comparable companies that have sold recently or whose value is public. For example, most small businesses in the UK sell at 2 times to 4 times profit before tax (PBT), with an average of 3 times. In the USA, it is common for small businesses (with a profit under £1m), to be valued at a multiple of Seller's Discretionary Earnings. SDE is a measure of all the financial resources the owner has at its disposal and equates to EBITDA + owner's salary + owner's private expenses passed through the company. According to Transworld, the US's largest broker, the accepted norm is to value a business at 2 times SDE.

The problem with using the comparables method is that it often leads owners to make an apples-to-oranges comparison. For example, a small medical device manufacturer might think that, because Smiths Group plc is trading for 23 times last year's earnings on the Stock Exchange, they too are worth 23 times last year's profit. However, if one compares with more common SME transactions, a small medical device manufacturer is likely to be sold close to 3x PBT.

Small companies are deeply discounted when compared to their FTSE 250 counterparts, so comparing your company with a giant will typically lead to disappointment. The huge valuations of quoted companies are linked to the liquidity premium these shares receive. The risk of owning highly illiquid small companies' shares is reflected in the value gap between quoted and unquoted shares.

A seller doesn't get to decide which method the buyer chooses. An acquirer will do the maths on what your business is worth to them in their office, with their professional advisers. They may decide your business is strategic, in which case they will be happy to pay more than comparable transactions. But in most cases, an acquirer will use a basic 3 times PBT multiple to value your company.

Where does this "3 times multiple" come from? Well, the buyers are limited by the banks in what they can offer for a business. Most lenders will lend a maximum of 2,5 times EBITDA. Given the fact that financial buyers don't want to risk too much of their own equity in one single deal, and given the risks inherent in owning a small business, if you want a 4, a 5 or a 6 times multiple, you will have to receive it on a deferred or conditional basis, and with flexible terms.

The million-pound mark

If you're wondering when is the best time to sell your company, you may want to wait until your company is generating £1 million in profit before tax. What's so special about the million-pound mark? It is a point at which the number of buyers interested in acquiring your business goes up dramatically. The more interested buyers you have, the better multiple of PBT you will command.

Since most small businesses are valued on a multiple of PBT, getting to a million in profits means you're not only getting a higher multiple but also applying your multiple to a larger number.

For example, according to industry statistics, a company with £200,000 in PBT might be valued at three times PBT, or £600,000. A company with a million pounds in PBT would be likely to command at least five times that figure, or £5 million. So, the company with £1 million in PBT is five times bigger than the £200,000 company, but almost 10 times more valuable.

There are a number of reasons that multiples go up with the level of profits and business size, including:

Deal costs

It costs about the same in legal and accounting fees to buy a company for £500,000 as it does to buy a company for £5 million. In large deals, these deal costs become a rounding error, but they amount to a comparatively larger share of the transaction on smaller deals.

The larger acquirer

In many trade deals, the acquiring company is between 5 and 20 times the size of the acquired company. More often than not, your natural acquirer, if you go the trade-buyer route, will indeed be between 5 and 20 times the size of your company.

If an acquiring business is less than 5 times your size, it is a risky proposition for the acquirer: If the acquisition fails, it will likely put the acquirer in dire straits.

If the acquirer is more than 20 times the size of your business, the acquirer will not enjoy a meaningful impact on his accounts by buying you. Most larger and mature companies look for a 10 to 20% turnover growth at a minimum. If they can get 5% of organic growth, they will try to acquire another 5% through acquisition, which means they need a target of sufficient size to make an impact.

Private Equity

Private equity firms are key acquirers of medium-sized businesses. The value of your company will increase if you're able to get a few such firms interested in buying you out. Yet most PE firms are looking for companies with at least £1 million in PBT. The £1m level is quite arbitrary, but very common. As with property buyers who narrow their Rightmove search to houses that fit within a price range, if you don't fit the minimum criteria, you may not be considered. If you're not very far off £1m in PBT and wanting to sell, you may want to make sure you pass the barrier, because the universe of buyers- and the multiple those buyers are willing to offer- increases when you reach it.

INTERVIEW

SHAUN KELLY

Corporate Finance BD Consultant,
Knights plc, a law firm

Maidstone

What is a typical multiple of profit before tax used for the valuation of an SME in the UK?

EBITDA multiple are often quoted as a very blunt valuation calculation in the Corporate Finance world and whilst it's true that an average (whatever that might be!), SME with a fair track record plus some potential might sell for 2-3x (larger ones for 4-5x), there are so many nuances that are always underpinned by the level of demand. Furthermore, once the enterprise value has been agreed, there is an adjustment on an equity basis (debt, surplus cash, etc.,) so there is no hard and fast formula here. In a nutshell, supply and demand always dictate and to generate strong demand and therefore improve the valuation it is incumbent upon an SME owner to invest time and effort in building an attractive asset.

The price (effectively the multiple), will generally be enhanced if the seller delivers what any investor/buyer wants and I generally parcel these requirements into the five following categories;

- Does the business have a deliverable growth plan that is broadly on target?
- Is the housekeeping in order - management information, contracts, etc.?
- Is there a spread of revenue streams (the more that is "sticky" or contracted the better!?)

- Can the business operate properly and successfully without the exiting parties/current owners?
- Does the business have a niche?

In my experience, deals generally fail because of a lack of realism and sale preparation from the seller's viewpoint and often from poor financial backing and structure re the buyer's side. SME owners should run their business, day to day, as if is being subjected to a buyer's due diligence. Always have the business in a fit state just in case an offer comes out of left field. Even if a buyer doesn't magically appear, then all those good pre-sale disciplines will ensure that the business performs with greater strength and sustainability.

A further point is that sellers often fail to plan for various exit strategies. A trade sale will often appear to be a straightforward strategy, but consider building a management team capable of fronting a buy-out, etc., etc.

Adjusting profits

Many owners want to know how they can improve their valuation. Obviously, your multiple will have a profound impact on the price of your business, but there is another number worthy of your consideration as well: the number your multiple is multiplying.

Most business owners think of profit as a tangible measure, calculated by a chartered accountant, but when it comes to the sale of your business, profit is far from objective. Your profit will go through a set of "adjustments" designed to estimate how profitable your company will be under a new owner.

This process of adjusting, and how you defend these adjustments to a buyer, can have a major impact on the price you agree with the buyer.

Say your business turns over £2 million and you pay yourself a salary of £200,000 a year. Further, let's assume the buyer could get a competent manager to run the business for him for £60,000 per year. You could therefore show the acquirer that under their ownership, your business would generate an extra £140,000 in profit. If they are paying you three times PBT for your business, that one adjustment has the potential to add an extra £700,000 to the price.

You should be able identify several adjustments that will increase your "normalised" profit and, by extension, the value of your business. You need to be prepared to prove each adjustment in order to show how profitable your company will be in the hands of a buyer.

Some of the most common adjustments relate to rent (common if your pension fund owns the unit your company operates from, and your company is paying over market rent), one-off lawsuits, pension contributions, one-time professional services fees, company cars, and other personal expenses run through the company's books.

The buyer can also come to you with adjustments in his favour. For instance, it is common in the UK for shareholders to pay themselves with a mix of salary and dividends. As the buyer will have to hire a paid MD to replace you, they will not be able to resort to dividends to pay this employee a part of their remuneration. Hence, they will have to subtract your own nominal salary from the profit before tax line and add back the market cost of your replacement.

If your company owns the property it occupies, its value will have to be added to your company's price, however the profits will have to be adjusted down for the rent the company will be paying the new property owner in the future.

Enterprise value and equity value

There is usually some confusion arising from these two terms. The enterprise value of your business is its intrinsic value, i.e. the price an investor is prepared to pay for the profit generation ability of an asset. The enterprise value is usually calculated by the DCF or the Comparables valuation methods.

The equity value is the price you are actually going to get from your shares. This is the enterprise value plus any assets which are surplus to the asset's profit-generation ability. Surplus assets include company-owned property, or surplus cash.

Surplus cash is the cash which is not necessary to the company's working capital cycle. This can be cash accumulated from retained earnings of past years.

If your company has debt, this will be subtracted from the Enterprise value of the company. For instance, if your company has an overdraft of £150K, and an enterprise value of £1m, the equity value will be £850K.

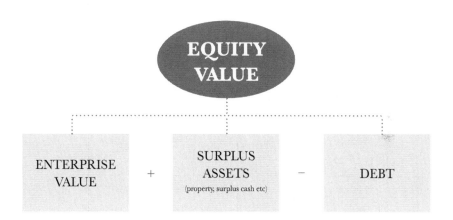

CHAPTER SEVEN

THE DEAL PROCESS

The offer

After having reviewed the information you provided them, the buyer will be ready to submit an offer, also called an indication of interest. This is typically communicated in written form, by email, or by post. The offer will outline the price as well as the terms that the buyer offers you. If you have set out an asking price, the offer is hopefully not too far off. Once you have received an offer, should you not accept it outright, you can make a counter offer, presenting the price and terms you are ready to accept; or you can stick to your guns and refer the buyer to your asking price and terms.

In order to save time going through an endless ballet of offers and counter offers, you may define a clear asking price, which is the valuation you or your corporate finance advisers ascribe to your business. The offer also includes a timeline for the transaction.

Although investors see an indication of interest as a serious document, they are non-binding. There are no guarantees in an offer at this stage. Actually, some buyers send out many offers every month as a way of seeing how the market is going and per chance have one of their offers accepted. It is also very common, especially with private equity firms, for a business owner to accept an attractive headline price, which will be chipped at during the due diligence stage. When you are reviewing an offer, it is helpful to understand the buyer's intentions. Is this a trade buyer on a spying exercise trying to get to the due diligence phase to learn as much as possible about your business? Is the buyer inexperienced and unlikely to be able to raise the necessary finance? Or have you met the investor several times, do you have good rapport with him, does he have a good reputation, and can you see yourself collaborating with this person?

USUAL QUESTIONS YOU WILL BE ASKED DURING THE PRE HEADS OF TERMS PHASE

The due diligence phase can be quite intimidating: the relentless barrage of questions fired at you from the potential buyer. Be prepared to be quizzed on all parts of your operations.

1. Why are you selling your business?

It's a difficult question. If your business really does have a huge potential - and you want the investor to believe that is the case - the obvious question is: "Why do you want to sell it, and do would you want to sell it now?"

2. What is your client-acquisition cost?

The potential acquirer wants to find out if you have a sales and marketing process which generates a certain amount of sales for each marketing pound you invest.

3. What is your market share?

The acquirer, with an eye on the potential, is trying to understand how big the potential market is for your product or services and what potential remains.

4. Who are the key members of staff?

The buyer wants to know the quality of your management team and determine specifically which members need to be included, motivated, and invested in after the deal closes.

5. Who buys your products and services?

Trade buyers will be looking for any possible synergies between what you sell and what they do. The more you know about your customer types, the better the acquirer will be able to determine the product fit. If your clients are businesses, a buyer will want to know what the role of your typical client is (e.g., PA, sales director, supply chain manager, MD), who buys your product or service.

6. How do you make your products and services?

The buyer is trying to work out if you have a secret formula in your production process, which a competitor would not be able to copy. They also want to make sure that the creation of your product or service is not dependent on any one person.

7. What is your USP?

A buyer is trying to understand how big the "moat" is around your business and what kind of protection it offers from other companies who may decide to compete with you in the future. What have you done to protect your business against all the other options the client has?

8. Can you describe your back-office setup?

Most buyers will try to understand how professional your administrative operation is. They will want to know what bookkeeping and billing software you use, how customers pay, and how you pay suppliers.

The terms

Setting an asking price is helpful and saves time; you can also go further, by outlining the terms you are ready to accept. For instance: "A total consideration of £1 million, with a minimum 60% initial consideration, and the rest payable on a 3-year deferred consideration. I am willing to stay 1 year as a consultant on £40K p.a. with Bupa health coverage and company car." A famous saying in the acquisition field is "you name the price; I choose the terms". Any local key-cutting shop could be sold for £38m with terms enabling the acquirer to pay the seller £1 a day.

It is helpful if you have an idea of the terms that you will and will not accept. For instance, how long are you happy to stay on after the sale? How much are you willing to accept on a deferred basis? Are you happy for a part of the consideration to be paid on an earn-out basis, i.e. subject to the business hitting certain targets? Your adviser, if you choose to retain one, will be able to steer you on these points.

The deferred consideration

It is quite typical that you won't receive a cheque for the whole price of your business and that you will be able to ride away into the sunset. Most deals include a deferred consideration, which can range from 30% to 60% of the price. Many sellers are not too reassured by the concept of a deferred consideration, and fear that the buyer will just find an excuse not to pay them. This is when your law firm comes in to keep a close eye on the drafting of the Heads of Terms and the Sale and Purchase agreement. You should be able to "claw back" your shares if ever the deferred payments aren't made.

Deferred consideration is always subordinated to bank debt. If the business doesn't generate enough cash flow to pay back the bank debt, the deferred consideration will not be paid either.

THE DEAL PROCESS

The earn-out

In most cases, you will get more money for your company if you are happy to stay on for some time to ensure that the handover goes well, and that your profit forecasts materialise in the future. It sounds simple, but in effect you are sharing the risk with the acquirer. Remember the forecasts you made to the buyer about your expected level of profits this current year, or the growth potential you suggested? Well the benefits of that, if they materialise, are likely to be paid out to you on a conditional basis in the future, i.e. in the form of an earn-out.

Even if you have a watertight earn-out agreement, there is always the risk of dealing with a dishonest buyer; even if you sue him, you may not get the results you anticipated when you signed the sale agreement. However if you have a good relationship with the buyer, if you both have a win-win mindset, and if the buyer has a good reputation in the market, an earn-out is a great way to bridge the gap between the company's value based on past profits and its future value based on growth potential.

Heads of Terms

Once you have an offer on the table, and both sides are happy with the terms, the next step is signing Heads of Terms, also known as a Letter of Intent. Most terms of a deal agreed in Heads of Terms are not binding; they help to formalise an agreement at one point in time, which will help each party clarify what they want from the deal. This Heads of Terms can then be used as a basis by the lawyers, when they prepare the Sale and Purchase agreement.

The Heads of Terms are an agreement to work towards a deal on the terms outlined, provided the facts you provided the investor are corroborated by the due diligence process.

The key thing that you are granting the buyer with signed Heads of Terms is exclusivity. Whereas before this you were free to talk with any potential buyer, you are now agreeing to stop all such conversations with any other investor.

So, make sure you are signing Heads of Terms with the Right One. The period of exclusivity can range from 60 to 120 days and obligates the seller to provide the information requested during this period.

It is also helpful to make sure, when you sign Heads of Terms, that the buyer can actually finance the transaction. Get them to staple to the draft document a written statement of a lender's willingness to provide debt, as well as a proof of funds from which the equity portion of the deal will be drawn. Due diligence costs money for both parties, and you also have opportunity costs by granting exclusivity to one seller. Make sure the buyer understands this if he is reluctant to provide proof of funds.

Other sections included in typical Heads of Terms include the price, the type of sale (stock or asset sale), the sources and uses of the funds, what needs to be done before the sale can take place, and a timeline on due diligence and steps.

Due diligence

Due diligence is the process during which the buyer tries to understand the particularities of your business, and hopefully uncover any liabilities or red flags before completion. Buyers are free to conduct as much or as little due diligence as they wish. However, if they are raising funds, the lender will typically insist on a full due diligence exercise.

Due diligence can be quite an intensive process for the company. The buyer, or their advisers, will go through checklists, requiring documents or explanations regarding many aspects of your business. As businesses don't usually have this information readily available, you will have to draw on the company's resources to put it together. Either you, or ideally a member of your team, will have to spend many hours finding, checking, and providing the information required.

This is why it is critical to have good books and records, ideally immediately available in a cloud- based ERP or accounting package. Your standard operating procedures manual, if you have one, will save a lot of time on both sides.

THE DEAL PROCESS

Due diligence covers three aspects:

- Legal due diligence is in general about confirming the general information about a company and its legal connections to other entities (clients, shareholders, etc.). It also confirms that the company is compliant to its regulatory environment. LDD also includes checking the legal basis of the company's assets and liability. Here are a few legal due diligence questions to give you an idea of what it entails:

  - Are the shareholders who they say they are?
  - Are there any disputes with the landlord?
  - Are the data-protection schedules adhered to?
  - Are the client contracts properly drafted?

- Financial due diligence gives the buyer assurances that the financials he has based his offer on accurately reflect the company's financial performance. When the financial due diligence team reviews the company's accounts, make sure they meet current generally accepted accounting practices (GAAP); provide for bad debts; calculate the value of stock appropriately; depreciate assets sensibly, etc. The due diligence team will also study the cash-flow cycle, invoicing terms, and collection procedures, especially if the buyer is looking to finance the receivables to raise funds. Here are a few typical financial due diligence questions:

  - How many days of turnover does the stock represent?
  - Do the accounts accurately reflect the bank statements?
  - What are the off-balance sheet liabilities?
  - Is tax properly accounted and paid? Are there any tax liabilities?

- Commercial due diligence looks at the strategic position of the business in the industry and explores the relationships your business has with suppliers and customers. The commercial due diligence also entails assessing the management team, identifying key staff and potential redundancies, and making sure you are not a liability to the business's future because of your relationships with key stakeholders. Here are a few typical commercial due diligence investigations:

- May I speak to your top 5 customers?
- May I meet with your 2 strategic suppliers?
- What would happen if the operations director left?

INTERVIEW

ANDREW GRIGGS
Senior Partner, Kreston Reeves
Corporate Finance Specialist
Chatham
www.krestonreeves.com

What do you look for during a financial due diligence exercise?
It really depends on the scope. One of the key things that we look for is a company's sustainable financial position: we want to make sure that the company is making profit and generating cash, achieving budget, delivering on its forecast, has its cash and working capital managed, and that suppliers are paid on time. Depending on the size of the business, we also look for adequate financial systems, controls, and procedures.

Have you ever found something in financial due diligence that has led you to advise your client to withdraw or change the terms of an agreed transaction?

Yes: if you look at inventory, for instance, and you find that they are holding a lot of unsellable old stock, you could argue that the business is overvalued. Similarly, if our team finds out that there is a significant tax liability or a history of poor payment to the tax authorities, the buyer could be founded to withdraw or to request a change in the terms of the deal.

What does financial due diligence look like?

Financial due diligence is tailored to every individual situation. First of all, we would agree with the buyer on the scope of our mission, and we will recommend what needs to be looked at. Then we compile a list of the information that we require and request it from the company or their advisers. We want to do as much work off-site as possible in order to cause as little distraction to the business as possible.

Sale and Purchase agreement

This document is a very long contract, probably the longest you will ever have to sign, and it is typically full of legal jargon. Your solicitor will be reviewing the sale and purchase agreement which is traditionally prepared by the buyer's solicitor. Your lawyer can therefore advise you on which parts of the agreement are critical, and which parts are boilerplate. All the parts of the SPA are negotiable, but it is preferable to have a pragmatic view and only focus on the key paragraphs, which should be, more or less, what you agreed at the Heads of Terms stage.

Make sure your lawyer is not being a deal killer, negotiating for the sake of negotiation. The best solicitors are pragmatic, commercially-minded professionals, who want to get the deal over the line whilst protecting your interests.

The principle of an SPA is simple: who is buying what, and at what price and when? In theory, an SPA is not necessary; you could sign over your share certificate in exchange for a cheque. However, the point of the document is to make sure the seller gets his money, and to make sure the buyer is protected from any hidden liabilities or risks.

These protections will take the form of a warranties and indemnities, and a disclosure letter. Is is also quite typical that the shareholders agree not to compete against their old company for a specific period of time and in a specific geographic region.

Completion is the meeting during which the sale and purchase agreement and stock transfer forms are signed. In addition, a series of documents usually need to be signed as well, including directors and shareholder meetings deciding on: resignation and appointment of directors, company secretary, change of registered office, change of accountants, bank mandates, and possibly a new memorandum and articles of association.

Once the SPA is signed, the lawyers will arrange the transfer of funds through their escrow accounts, and the first payment should appear in your bank account, once your professional fees are paid for.

And then starts the next chapter of your life.

ALEX PAWLE

I am a business owner and investor based near Ashford, Kent, UK.

I started a B2B company in 2003 which has now grown to 35 employees, with strong sales and healthy profits as well as an amazing management team. We are proud of our ISO-9001 certification, which we take seriously. I have increased the profit before tax regularly, every year. I sold this company in June 2019.

The journey to becoming the business owner I am today has been at times exhilarating, tedious, stressful and fun. But it is a journey that taught me much and made me many great friends. I am proud to have created a business that operates and grows without me, whilst retaining my values and vision.

I am partnering with local investor Stephane Leduc to invest in UK industry, starting in Kent. Using the funds from the recent sales of our businesses, we are investing and acquiring industrial companies in Kent and Sussex, and growing them to become national champions. We are not giving up on manufacturing in the UK and in Europe. Quite the contrary. Let's switch-on our machine-tools and carry on manufacturing and exporting.

The acquirer of Alex's company, Steven Thépaut, said:

"From a tiny office in 2003 with a phone/fax machine and second hand computers as sole assets, to the current state of Mot-Tech as a very profitable, well run, ISO-9001 company, with 35 full time employees, we have covered a lot of ground. Alex is to thank for most of the improvements in the processes we have undergone during these past 15 years. He transformed us from a fledgling moth of a business into a profitable company, and am grateful for having learnt with him, all these years, how to do good business. Alex also has been a respectful negotiating partner in our current MBO. He has been fair on valuation and has worked hard with me to get to a win-win situation that works for everyone. I recommend him to a business seller as a safe pair of hands for your business. Please write to me for more information about Alex on: s.thepaut@mot-tech.com".

Steven, a happy business buyer, signing the acquisition of Alex's company, surrounded by bankers

MEET

STEPHANE LEDUC

Stephane Leduc is a French business owner and investor. He moved from France to the UK in 2013. He started a book publishing business in Paris with his father in 2002. Along the tagline « books for a better life », the company grew rapidly with a double-digit yearly growth for over 15 years. The company was sold in December 2018 to the French publishing titan Albin Michel. Stephane is currently Alex's partner in Kent Business Investors.

Stephane lives in Whitstable, with his wife and 3 children.

INVESTMENT FIRM MOVES FOR PRECISION METALWORKING BUSINESS

l-r: Alex Pawle, Lee Huntley and Stephane Leduc

An Ashford-based provider of high precision sheet metalworking services has been acquired by Kent Business Investors.

Pegasus Precision has been acquired from former owner, Lee Huntley, who intends to stay involved for the foreseeable future to help the company expedite its growth and support its customers. All employees are also expected to remain with Pegasus.

"Through the acquisition of Pegasus Precision, we have decided to invest in industry, in particular in our home counties of Kent and East Sussex," said Stephane Leduc, director of Kent Business Investors.

"We believe that the time has come to fund industry and to relocalise high added value manufacturing in the UK."

Alex Pawle, director of Kent Business Investors, added: "Pegasus Precision struck us as a highly specialised manufacturer with very skilled staff and strong customer relationships. We look forward to preserving the company founder's legacy and building on his philosophy of continuous improvement and manufacturing excellence."

Lee Huntley, Pegasus Precision founder, said: "I am glad to have reached a win-win done deal with Alex and Stephane for their investment in my company. Throughout the process, they were attentive to us reaching an arrangement through which both parties could benefit equally. I look forward to staying very much involved and working on Pegasus Precision's success over the long term."

Along with other local investors, Kent Business Investors will be deploying its funds to acquire and grow other high quality industrial companies, in Kent and Sussex.

To talk to Alex and Stephane about selling your business,
call 01227 314 072 or write to a.pawle@kentbusinessinvestors.co.uk
or visit www.kentbusinessinvestors.co.uk

HOW TO SELL YOUR BUSINESS IN KENT & SUSSEX

ALEX PAWLE

KENT BUSINESS
INVESTORS

LET'S INVEST IN INDUSTRY

Printed in Great Britain
by Amazon